Discovering the PAST

S0-ANP-719

A READ-ABOUT

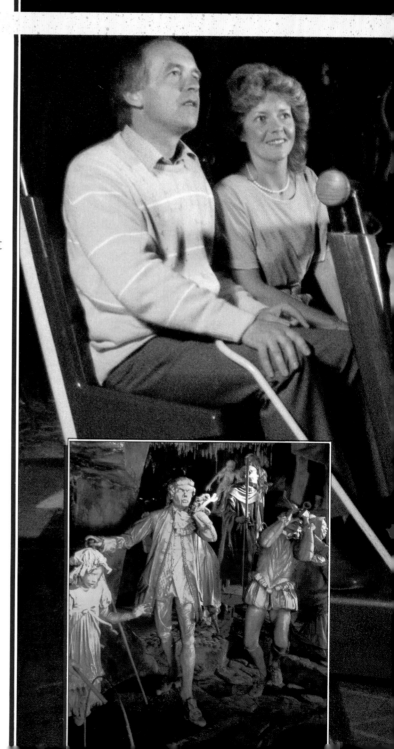

We talk about the past, the present, and the future. But the present is only a fleeting moment, a succession of events that are always changing, while the future is unknown.

The past is different. It is always there. But it is only meaningful if events and details are recorded; for as time goes by we humans either forget what happened or fail to pass the information on to the next generation.

In hundreds of years' time most of our things will have been lost or destroyed, but a few may remain. For the people who live in the future they will provide clues about how we lived and what we did.

By using similar clues from the past, we can discover what the world was like and how people lived many years ago.

*i*f you go to the city of York in northern England, you can do just that. For there, at the Jorvik Viking Centre, you can sit in a special car and glide back a thousand years in time.

Your time car takes you slowly backwards through a time tunnel that will eventually lead you to part of the tenth-century settlement of Jorvik, cleverly recreated by a skilled team of designers, builders, artists, sound and lighting technicians, and many others.

You leave the sights and sounds of the twentieth century and pass generation after generation of people who once lived in York. At first, you see discarded toys similar to those once owned by your grandparents and great-grandparents. You pass a young Victorian girl playing with a hoop, and an old lady selling vegetables.

Further and further back into the past you go, watching and listening as minstrels play their songs and medieval street traders sell their wares. At one stage, you see a weeping mother carrying the body of her baby that has been killed by the terrible plague called the Black Death.

Suddenly you seem to enter a fiery furnace, where wooden houses are burning and people are crying out in a strange language. Then, unharmed, you come out into bright sunshine to find yourself in the old Viking settlement of Jorvik, just as it was on a late October afternoon in the year AD 948.

You travel down the ancient street of Coppergate to experience the sights, sounds and smells of that ancient settlement and see some of the townspeople as they buy and sell, work, sit at home or play.

You already know of Coppergate, for before you left the twentieth century it was one of the streets that you had walked down in York. But now it is quite different. Gone are all the stone and brick buildings, and instead you are looking at low wooden houses covered in thatch. The street is narrow and there is no paving, just dried mud.

The language of the inhabitants is in a foreign dialect that you can't understand. Yet, although the place feels strange, there are familiar sounds.

A dog is barking outside one of the thatched houses, and inside, a baby is crying. You can hear people talking and laughing. Like the sounds, the smells are both familiar and unfamiliar. Instead of vehicle exhausts or factory smoke, there are the scents of leather, freshly spun wool, wood smoke and cooked meat.

From time to time there are also unpleasant smells, and you realize that they are caused by decomposing carcasses and human and animal excrement.

There is no such thing as a sewage system here, and rubbish is just thrown out behind the houses to rot. The toilet is a hole in the ground, surrounded by a low woven fence.

You peer into the houses as you pass. You watch Thorfast carve antler bone into implements and ornaments. Across the road, Lothin is doing business at his jewellery stall – although by the look on the woman customer's face, his prices could be a little high!

You pass a house where a man is making wooden bowls and barrels. This man is called a cooper. Many of today's surnames are derived from the occupations of our ancestors. The name Cooper, like that of Smith, is very common.

Now your time machine takes you right inside a Viking home. You see an old man talking to two women, one of whom is putting sticks on the fire that smokes in the middle of the room. They are preparing the evening meal.

In one corner is a bed covered in skins, and you realize that the whole of their home life is spent in this one room.

A small boy and a girl chatter together as they watch their mother weave on a simple loom. No school for them! They learn everything from the members of their family and the other people in the street.

Down at the wharf, men unload a cargo of furs, wine and herring from a wooden cargo boat that has just arrived from Norway. Another man mends its sail.

Two men called Karl and Edmund gut fish. A young boy, Toki, listens to their stories of Viking exploits.

Almost before you know it, you are back in the twentieth century. It is now 1980 and you are watching people excavate the remains of a Viking village. Yes, it is the one through which you have just travelled, looking as it did when it was first discovered.

You can see the remains of the wooden house walls, some now barely recognizable, others still well preserved and at least a metre (3 feet) high. You notice that things are being examined, measured, labelled and photographed before being removed.

Parts of buildings have been carefully preserved, labelled and put back as they were found.

Your time car moves on, and suddenly you are back in the present day. You step out and enter a museum, where items found during the dig are displayed. By looking at these, and at various photographs and displays, you learn more about Jorvik (the old Viking name for today's York). You also learn how archaeologists discovered it and brought it to the world's attention.

This helmet and the tenth-century coin die, lead trial pieces and silver pennies (left) were dug up at Jorvik and are now displayed in the Jorvik Viking Centre museum.

*t*he people who discovered Jorvik are called archaeologists, and the excavation that they carried out is called a dig.

Archaeologists study history by looking at things left from the past. These may have been made by people, or they may be natural things like plant or animal remains, soil, fossils or rocks.

Things that were made by people are called artefacts. The most common materials used in the making of artefacts were wood, shell, stone, bone or metal.

Only those artefacts made of the harder materials are likely to be found, because those made from softer materials will probably have rotted away.

The dig described at Jorvik was an exception. The area lay between the junction of two rivers, and the damp ground preserved some of the objects made from softer materials. So the archaeologists found quite large remains of house timbers, together with artefacts like wooden bowls and leather shoes.

Archaeologists aren't the only people who search for the past. Other experts include geologists, who study soils and rocks and the fossils in them; botanists, who study plants; and biologists, who study animal life.

These archaeologists are working on a dig. On the right are some of their finds. Those in the right front corner are natural objects. Around them are artefacts, or objects made by people.

These amber beads, and the bone and antler combs, pins, spindle whorls and fabrics (top right), were made in the tenth century. So were the old wooden bowls (bottom right), which once looked like the modern replicas. All were found at Jorvik.

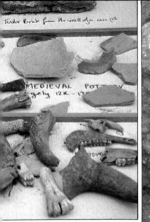

Tudor Brick from the wall of a cess pit

MEDIEVAL POT—
legely 12K—13

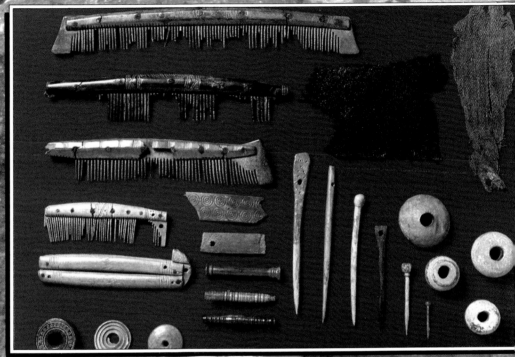

THE SEARCH FOR CLUES

*a*rchaeologists use certain surface features as clues in their search for digging sites. These include things like mounds, depressions, or ancient monuments that show that people might once have lived nearby.

Both on land and at sea, old remains usually get covered over with mud, dirt or other debris that accumulate over the years, and can be up to 10 metres (33 feet) deep.

Erosion by wind and rain can uncover objects. For example, a geologist found a tiny piece of bone protruding from a cliff in a valley in New Zealand. Further digging revealed that the bone was in fact part of the nose of a large whale. Behind it lay the whale's skull and the rest of the skeleton. The whale was about 9 metres (30 feet) long and is thought to have died about 30 million years ago.

Excavations for buildings, dams, or road and rail cuttings, can also unearth objects. They may also reveal many different layers of soil or rock, piled one upon another. Each of these layers, called strata, indicates a particular period of time.

Archaeologists also rely on old reports, books or pictures to tell them what went on many years ago. The careful records they keep when they do discover something help them to plan further searches.

Aerial photography is also used. Sometimes it can show up differences in colour that outline the positions of old walls, ditches and roads. Another aerial technique is the use of an infra-red camera.

Before searching for shipwrecks, people first read old reports and books put together from the stories of survivors. These may help to identify the place where a ship sank.

This aerial photograph cle[arly] human activity. The pict[ure] some of these terraces [...] They would once have [...] in the reconstruction pic[ture] guard the settlement on [...]

Here you can see the different layers, or strata, in the rocks.

...s signs of
... shows how
... the ground.
...sades like those
... left), to
... of the hill.

Pictures like this old lithograph of Gloucester help us to see what life was like in the past.

EXCAVATION

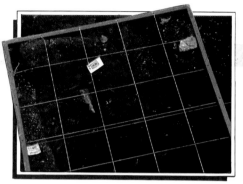

The large, numbered site squares are further subdivided with a small, portable grid like this.

This old well is almost in its original state.

archaeologists plan each search very carefully. First they draw a map of the part they want to explore. Then they draw lines dividing the map into squares, and each square is given a reference number.

Next, they use a strong cord to divide the *site* into squares corresponding to those on the site *map*. They label each of these squares to match the map. They then hammer survey pegs into the ground and mark them with the "ground level" from which the dig starts. This enables the depth of the dig to be measured later.

Now excavation starts. In many cases the soil will be in strata or "time layers", which can be recognized by their colour and the type of material they contain. Using a technique called "stratigraphy", the archaeologists work their way down, one layer at a time, getting all the information they can before going on to the next. You could compare it to peeling the layers off an onion.

They remove every bit of dirt or rubble very carefully so as not to damage anything underneath, then sieve and examine it. If the soil is damp, it may need to be dried first. In this way even the smallest remains are found.

Diggers carefully uncover a

abels indicate different strata, or time

they come across.

The "finds" are later cleaned and sorted.

When a buried object is found, it is partly excavated, then labelled and photographed. Measurements, notes and drawings are made recording its exact position within a particular square, and its exact depth below ground level.

After that it is removed and taken to a "finds shed" for cleaning and further examination.

If a layer appears interesting, the archaeologists may start to dig outwards, to see what else they can find in that layer. They may find old post holes showing the former sites of houses, a well, a drain, a grain pit or a grave. Clues like these help them to work out what they call the "settlement pattern", which in turn will give further clues as to where to dig next.

A PICTURE EMERGES

What a lot of finds to sort!

When you try to solve a jigsaw puzzle, you start off with a picture of what it should look like and hundreds of different pieces. As you examine each piece you look at the pattern and colours on it and compare these with the master picture. You also look at its shape, and for pieces that could fit into it. Gradually, through trial and error, you build up the whole picture.

Archaeologists don't have a master picture to work from, but they do have the pieces of the puzzle in the form of the objects that they find.

First they send every item they find for identification by experts. It is compared with similar objects which have a known history. If it doesn't fit a known pattern, then other experts may be asked to look at it.

For example, if the object is made of an unusual type of stone, then a geologist may be called in to suggest where that sort of stone may have come from, and where the object may have been made.

It may even be necessary to get help from another country, as happened when a Spanish helmet over 300 years old was dredged up in a bay in New Zealand.

As each item is identified and recorded on a master chart, the diggers get a better idea of the overall picture and what they are excavating.

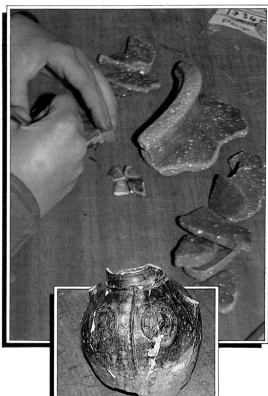

Sometimes enough broken pieces can be found to reconstruct an item like the old burial urn (inset).

Every item is carefully studied and labelled.

Many of the finds are what we today would call junk: things that people no longer used, or had broken and thrown away.

As these artefacts are collected, cleaned, preserved and identified, a broader picture develops. For example, in one part of the Jorvik dig many pieces of leather were found, along with some old shoes and a couple of shoemaker's lasts. The archaeologists concluded that the area had been the site of a shoemaker's shop.

Some objects are so small that they need to be examined under a microscope. This can reveal the remains of beetles and other insects, and the seeds from all sorts of different plants.

Eventually all the pieces of the puzzle come together to form a picture of what life was like at that particular time compared with today. The archaeologists learn how the people used to live and work, and how they coped with their environment.

by identifying and dating the fossilized remains of plants and animals, scientists have been able to build up a picture of what life was like millions of years ago. They have devised a time-scale showing when certain plants and animals first developed, and when some of them eventually became extinct.

They have concluded that the earliest forms of life started in the sea. Simple plants were the first forms of life on land, which was not colonized by animals until millions of years later.

One puzzle still to be solved is why the dinosaurs disappeared. From the study of fossils, we know that those land reptiles were once the largest and most powerful creatures on earth. We know how big they were, what the various species looked like, and what sort of plants or animals they ate. But we still do not know for sure why the dinosaurs suddenly became extinct.

The answer may now be closer. Recently, Chinese geologists examined a huge crater, 80 kilometres (50 miles) in diameter, which was discovered in one of the most inaccessible parts of Inner Mongolia. They have decided that the crater was made by a huge meteorite which hit the earth about 136 million years ago, at the time that the dinosaurs are thought to have become extinct.

They suggest that the huge dust clouds thrown up by the tremendous collision blotted out the sun and created an artificial winter. This, combined with very little light, caused most of the plants to die. Many of the dinosaurs were vegetarian and, without plants to eat, they slowly starved to death. In turn the flesh-eating dinosaurs ran out of food and they too died.

SUNKEN TREASURE

These treasures were all recovered from sunken ships.

*n*ot all searches occur on land. Divers also search the sea bed and look for shipwrecks which may contain interesting artefacts.

Inventions like the aqualung and battery-powered scooters have given people a lot more opportunity to search for sunken ships. The use of undersea robots called remote-operated vehicles (R.O.V.s) has greatly improved the chances of finding them. An R.O.V. was used to search for the wreck of the liner *Titanic*, which sank on 14 April 1912, in the North Atlantic, after hitting an iceberg while on its maiden voyage.

This true story shows the sort of thing that divers may find if they are lucky. In about AD 1650, a Chinese trading junk loaded up with a cargo of blue-and-white Ming porcelain set sail for Jakarta, in the country that is now called Indonesia. (Dutch ships used to call at this port to pick up cargo for their trade with Europe.)

The junk never completed the journey. Perhaps a typhoon struck: we don't know. Whatever happened, the ship sank in the South China Sea and took its precious cargo to the bottom. There, 40 metres (131 feet) below the surface, still packed in boxes and surrounded by rice straw, the fragile porcelain items lay undisturbed for over 330 years.

The wreck was discovered by a man who earned his living by searching for sunken World War II

Treasure isn't always gold or jewels.

ships and salvaging them for scrap. The cargo didn't contain any jewels or gold, but the porcelain sold for millions of pounds. It really did turn out to be buried treasure.

The lure of buried treasure also attracts irresponsible treasure-hunters who pull everything apart, breaking or throwing away the things they consider useless and keeping only those likely to earn them some money.

They destroy information that would be of great value to archaeologists. In some cases, the things they destroy are more valuable than the things they keep. Shipwrecks are particularly attractive to treasure-hunters, because many old ships carried precious items such as gold and jewels.

BE A DETECTIVE

You don't have to be an expert to play detective. Here are a few examples of what you can do.

USE MUSEUMS

If you live in a town or city, you may be able to visit a museum. Many countries have a national museum, which specializes in collecting things to do with that country. There are also local museums, which show items collected in the district, and may put on displays that tell you the history of the area.

Museums collect things, many of which are given by people or purchased with money that has been donated. They often restore these to make them as close as possible to their original condition.

But museums don't collect just anything. The people who run museums choose special things that they think are important. These include natural things like rocks and plant or animal remains, objects made and used by humans, and written or spoken material. Museums collect things from today as well as from the past, keeping them safe for future generations to enjoy.

It is no good collecting things if people can't see them. So museums put them out for people to look at. They take great care to display their collections in the right way, making them interesting to look at, while keeping them safe.

Many of the items are very fragile or valuable, and must be protected from people touching them. That is why so many are kept in glass cases.

Some specialist museums even have live exhibits. This sheep is one of the old breeds of animal on display at a farm museum in England.

Light can also damage things, especially those made from natural materials. It must therefore be carefully controlled.

Most museums are divided into areas, each specializing in a particular type of object. One area may be devoted to pottery, glassware and ceramics; another to geology, showing how rocks, mountains, volcanoes and rivers were formed, and showing animal and plant fossils.

There are usually areas devoted to art, and others to natural history, displaying not only plants and animals that can be found today but also models of extinct animals, like the dinosaurs. Some areas may display different methods of transport, such as horse-drawn vehicles, bicycles, trams and old motor vehicles.

Some museums specialize in just one thing, such as old trains, aircraft or machinery.

Museums can be fun, too. Many of them put on special exhibitions and guided tours for children.

If what you are interested in is not on display, ask a museum attendant. Museums often keep a large number of items in storage. Some of these may be shown occasionally in special exhibitions, but many are available for people to study at other times.

Researchers study museum objects to try to find out more about them. We have already learned how some of them studied the objects found at York and were able to put the facts together to tell the story about life in Jorvik. Researchers also write articles about their findings to share their knowledge with others.

OTHER PLACES TO LOOK

Something you pick up in a curio shop could start **your** journey into the past.

ou can learn a lot about the past by visiting art galleries. Pictures drawn or painted many years ago can show you people's appearance, what their houses and furniture looked like, and many other details about their lives.

Old photographs are also a good source of information. Look in your library for suitable books, old newspapers and old magazines.

Find a cutting or cliff face where you can see soil or rock strata. Make notes and drawings, then try to identify their age. You may be able to enlist the help of a geologist or find a geological map of the area.

Look for a large tree stump and try to age it by counting the number of growth rings. Then see if you can find out more about the sort of trees that grew in your neighbourhood before people started to live there. Perhaps it was a forest; or maybe it was a desert with no trees at all.

Some people enjoy putting together their family tree. You may like to trace your ancestors back as far as you can. You need the help of as many relatives as possible, such as parents, grandparents, great-grandparents, uncles and aunts. There could also be family friends who would help.

Find out as much as you can about your own home. If the house belongs to your family, locate the deeds or title. This will tell you who owned it, and when. Try to trace back to the time it was first built.

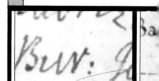

People tracing their family
useful information in the re
deaths and marriages kept

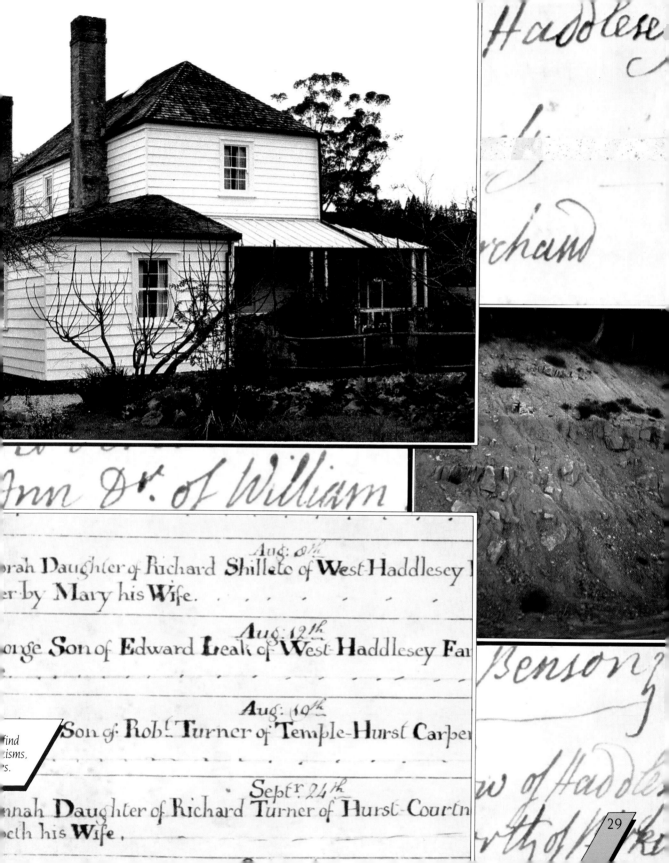

Haddlese

chard

Inn Dr. of William

...rah Daughter of Richard **Shillete** of **West Haddlesey**
...er by **Mary** his **Wife**. . . . . . .

Aug: 8th

Aug: 19th

...orge **Son** of Edward **Leak** of **West Haddlesey** Fa...

Aug: 19th

...Son of Robt. **Turner** of **Temple-Hurst** Carpe...

find
...isms,
...s.

Septr. 24th

...nnah **Daughter** of Richard **Turner** of **Hurst-Courtn**...
...eth his **Wife**. .

Benson

...w of Haddle...
...rth of...

29

The author dug up these bottles in his garden. They were in a place where people threw their rubbish many years ago.

Search for old objects in your garden. Quite often you can unearth interesting things merely by digging in your own backyard. For example, try to locate where an old rubbish pile was, and search there.

Talk to old people. Many of them can tell you stories about what it used to be like when they were children. This information, together with that discovered in old books and magazines, will help you picture what life used to be like in your area.

Stamp and money collections provide further clues to the past. Some stamps were printed to commemorate events; others to depict famous people. Many countries produce sets of stamps with a particular theme, such as old trains or aircraft.

Look around you. Study old buildings and historic places, and learn about the period in which they were built and the people who built them. Look at monuments and learn why they were built. Study the old headstones in cemeteries. Visit curio and antique shops, and see what interesting things you can find.

In fact, one of these shops could provide a good starting point for your own search for the past. You could choose an object that interests you and find out as much as you can about it and the period in which it was made and used.

However you choose to start, there's no knowing where your search might end, once you begin discovering the past.

INDEX